THE STRANGE VOYAGE
OF MÁEL DÚIN

THE STRANGE VOYAGE OF
MÁEL DÚIN

A Journey to the Otherworld

COMPILED AND EDITED BY DAVID MAJOR

ILLUSTRATED BY MIDJOURNEY

A DISTANT MIRROR

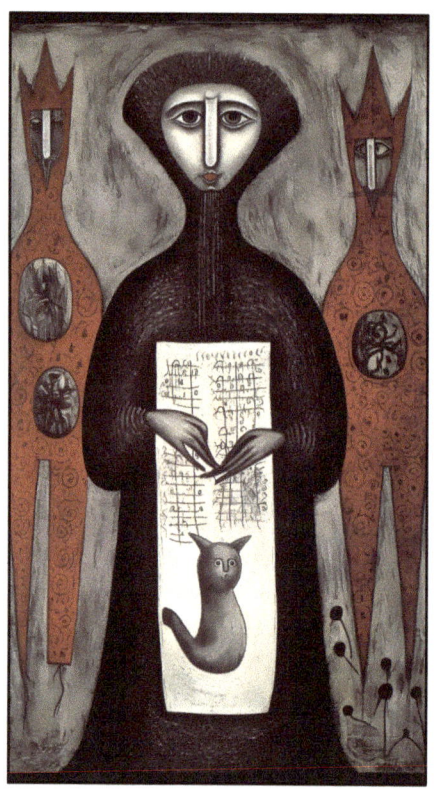

THE STRANGE VOYAGE OF MÁEL DÚIN
A Journey to the Otherworld

© 2023 A Distant Mirror

ISBN 978-0-6488705-7-9

Compiled and edited by David Major
dm@adistantmirror.com

Illustrations by Midjourney
midjourney.com

All rights to this edition of this work are reserved. No part of this book may be reproduced or transmitted in any form or by any means, graphic, electronic, or mechanical, without the permission of the publisher.

Email: contact@adistantmirror.com

Web: adistantmirror.com

It is in vain to dream of a wildness distant from ourselves.

There is none such.

It is the bog in our brains and bowels, the primitive vigor of Nature in us, that inspires that dream.

– HENRY DAVID THOREAU

THE STRANGE VOYAGE OF MÁEL DÚIN

1. The Warrior and the Nun / 17
2. The Birth of Máel Dúin / 19
3. The Death of Ailill Ócar Agha / 21
4. Máel Dúin Grows Up / 23
5. Máel Dúin Learns the Truth / 25
6. Máel Dúin Meets His Father's People / 29
7. Máel Dúin Builds a Currach and Sets Sail / 32
8. The Island of the Murderers / 36
9. The Ants / 41
10. Many Brightly Colored Birds / 43
11. The Beast that Threw Stones / 44
12. The Demonic Horse Race / 47
13. The Palace of Solitude / 51
14. The Great Apple Tree / 53
15. The Wondrous Creature / 55
16. The Bloodthirsty Horses / 59
17. The Fiery Swine / 61
18. The Little Cat / 66
19. The Island of the Sheep / 69
20. The Burning River and the Herdsman / 71
21. The Mill / 75
22. The Island of Sorrow / 79

23. The Four Fences / 83

24. The Palace of the Glass Bridge / 85

25. The Shouting Birds / 91

26. The Hermit / 93

27. The Miraculous Fountain / 97

28. The Blacksmiths / 99

29. The Sea of Glass / 103

30. The Country Beneath the Waves / 105

31. A Prophecy / 109

32. The Arch of Water / 113

33. The Silver Pillar / 115

34. The Pedestal / 119

35. The Island of Women / 121

36. The Fruit / 129

37. The Three Eagles / 131

38. The Laughing Folk / 139

39. The Wall of Fire / 141

40. The Monk of Toraigh / 143

41. The Falcon / 159

42. The Homecoming / 161

The Strange Voyage of Máel Dúin is a legendary tale from Irish Gaelic literature that holds a significant place in the traditions of myth and history. It recounts the extraordinary maritime journey of the eponymous hero Máel Dúin and his companions as they embark on a perilous quest.

The story begins with Máel Dúin seeking revenge for the death of his father at the hands of raiders. He gathers a crew of seventeen warriors (plus three stepbrothers who decide to tag along) and sets sail in a currach, a small Irish boat.

Their voyage takes them through various mystical islands and encounters with fantastic beings, testing their courage, wit, and resilience.

Throughout the voyage, Máel Dúin and his crew face a series of challenges and adventures. They encounter strange islands inhabited by giant birds, shape-shifting creatures, sea monsters, and other supernatural beings. Each encounter requires the crew to demonstrate their bravery and resourcefulness, often relying on their own intuition, as well as guidance from a variety of mentors and advisers.

One of the prominent themes is the pursuit of vengeance. Máel Dúin's quest for revenge initially drives the narrative, reflecting the importance of honor and justice in Irish Gaelic culture. However, as the story progresses, Máel Dúin learns the value of forgiveness and the limitations of seeking retribution, ultimately choosing a path of reconciliation and mercy.

The Strange Voyage of Máel Dúin is a rich tapestry that weaves together elements of mythology, folklore, and historical references. It incorporates motifs found in other Irish legends, such as the Otherworld, a realm of supernatural beings parallel to our own, as well as the concept of the heroic quest. The tale also draws inspiration from the seafaring traditions of ancient Ireland and showcases the knowledge of seafaring and maritime skills of the time.

As an integral part of Irish Gaelic tradition, *The Strange Voyage of Máel Dúin* serves several purposes. It entertains with its surreal and adventurous elements, capturing the imagination of its audience. It also reflects the cultural values of the time, emphasizing the importance of honor, loyalty, and the pursuit of justice. Moreover, the story embodies the enduring oral tradition of passing down tales from generation to generation, preserving the history, myth, and wisdom of the Irish people.

The main text was compiled and edited by David Major.
The illustrations are by Midjourney, versions 5 to 5.2.
This introduction was written by ChatGPT.

A world that does not include Utopia is not even worth glancing at, for it leaves out the one country at which Humanity is always landing.

And when Humanity lands there, it looks out, and seeing a better country, sets sail.

— OSCAR WILDE

THE STRANGE VOYAGE
OF MÁEL DÚIN

1. THE WARRIOR AND THE NUN

LONG AGO, there lived among the Eoganacht clan of Ninuss, in the kingdom of Thomond, a warrior named Ailill Ócar Agha.[1]

He was a hero and a chief among his clan and family, and he was famed as a brave fighter.

The King of Thomond was leading a raid into Kildare, and Ailill and his clansmen accompanied him.

There, they camped one night near a church, beside which was a convent of nuns.

During the night, while the camp was quiet, Ailill went near the church. When the young prioress of the convent came out to ring the bell for nocturns, Ailill seized her, threw her down on to the ground, and raped her.

"But we are in an unblessed state!" the young nun cried, "and this is the time of my conceiving! What is your tribe, and what is your name?" she pleaded. "Who are you?"

"I am Ailill Ócar Agha," he boasted, "and I am chief of the Eoganacht of Ninuss!" And he left her in tears by the church, and did not care whether she would become pregnant or not.

The King of Thomond continued his raid, until he had done enough. Then he took his army back to Thomond, and Ailill Ócar Agha and his clansmen went with him.

---

[1] or 'Ailill of the Edge of Battle'

2. THE BIRTH OF MÁEL DÚIN

In time, the young prioress bore a son, and she named him Máel Dúin.

Now, she knew that she could not keep the child; and as she was a friend of the Queen of the kingdom of Aran, she took her baby there.

"Take my child," she begged the Queen. "Please, raise him as your own, for I cannot."

Now the Queen of Aran loved her friend dearly, and so she agreed, and she took the baby, and raised Máel Dúin as her son, along with her own children.

3. THE DEATH OF AILILL ÓCAR AGHA

Not long after Máel Dúin had been taken into the royal household by the good Queen of Aran, the Eoganacht of Ninuss were attacked in their homes by raiders from Leix, in the kingdom of Loígis.

Ailill's house was surrounded, and he fled for shelter to a church named Dooclone. The raiders followed him there, and slew him in the church, and then burned it down over his body.

The ruins of the church are there to this day.

And so Ailill Ócar Agha of the Eoganacht lived and died, but left a son in the world.

4. MÁEL DÚIN GROWS UP

Máel Dúin was raised with the three sons of the King and Queen of Aran, as if he was one of their own.

He slept in the same room with them, and was fed from the same breast and the same plate, and drank from the same cup.

He had the same tutors, and played the same games.

And he was a lovely child; everyone who saw him had no doubt that there could be no other child in the world who was as beautiful in either body or spirit as was the young Máel Dúin.

He was high-spirited and generous, and he loved all sorts of manly exercises. In ball-playing, in running and leaping, in throwing, in chess, in rowing, and in horse-racing, he surpassed all the youths that came to the palace, and he won every contest.

As he grew up to be a young man, the noble qualities of his mind gradually bloomed, and he became expert in legends, and histories, and poetry, so that soon he knew all the stories of his people.

There was no other young man like Máel Dúin, in all the lands of the Eoganacht.

5. MÁEL DÚIN LEARNS THE TRUTH

ONE DAY, the youths of the royal court were at play, competing among themselves in tests of strength and skill. Máel Dúin was winning every contest, and at last one of his companions, consumed with envy, burst out in anger and frustration:

"To think that you, whose clan and kin no one knows, whose father and mother no one knows, can beat us in every game of skill and strength, on land or on water, on horseback or on the chess board! What shame for us, we who are born to royalty!"

And the others who were there agreed, and they all laughed at Máel Dúin.

On hearing this, Máel Dúin ceased his playing, and stood in silence, deep in thought, for until then, he had believed that he was the son of the King and Queen, and that their three sons were truly his beloved brothers.

Confused and surprised, he went to the Queen.

"Who are my mother and father? I will neither eat nor drink until you tell me the truth!"

"Why are you asking me that?" said the Queen. "Pay no heed to the jealous nonsense that your brothers speak. I am your mother, for no mother ever loved her son more than I love you!"

"I do not doubt your love, and I also love you," replied Máel Dúin. "But I must know who my parents are. So please, tell me!"

And as Máel Dúin insisted on knowing the truth, the Queen at last took him to meet his mother.

The prioress and her son greeted each other with great emotion, and many tears.

Máel Dúin then asked his mother about his father.

"My dear son," she said, "it will make you no happier to know who he was, nor will it in any way profit you. He has been dead for many years, and it is no loss to the world."

"Be that as it may," replied the youth, "but it is better for me that I know. I must know, mother!"

And so the prioress relented, and told her son.

"Máel Dúin, your father was none other than Ailill Ócar Agha, the chief of the Eoganacht, of Ninuss."

6. MÁEL DÚIN MEETS HIS FATHER'S PEOPLE

Soon afterwards, Máel Dúin traveled with his three foster brothers to Ninuss, where his father's people lived.

He was greeted warmly and made welcome, and so much honor was shown to the four visitors that soon they became happy and content, and Máel Dúin forgot all the abasement and trouble that had led him there.

He heard many stories and memories of his father.

One day, it happened that a number of young men were in a churchyard, amusing themselves. The game was to compete in throwing stones clear over the charred roof of the church, for it had been burned many years ago, and Máel Dúin was there, taking part.

Máel Dúin was about to cast his stone, and to steady himself, he placed his foot on a scorched flagstone.

A fellow named Briccne, a monk attached to the church, was close by, and he said to Máel Dúin:

"It would be better for you to avenge the man who was burned to death here, rather than amuse yourself by throwing stones over his poor burnt bones!"

"Who was burned here?" asked Máel Dúin.

"Why, this is the Dooclone church," replied the monk, and the one who was slain here was your own father! It was Ailill Ócar Agha who died on the very rock on which you are now resting your foot!"

"Who slew him?" asked Máel Dúin.

"Raiders from Leix attacked us. They slew our chief, your father, and they burned this very church over his body," replied Briccne. "And they are still sailing," he added. "Even today, they are still committing their crimes."

On hearing this, Máel Dúin dropped the stone that he had been holding. He fastened his cloak around him, and buckled on his shield.

He left the gathering at Dooclone church, and from then on he asked everyone he met whether they knew anything about the raiders from Leix.

For a long time, he could find no news of them; but finally he met some merchants who knew where the raiders' fleet lay. They told him that the raiders' home was a great distance away – and that to reach it would require a long and dangerous sea voyage.

7. MÁEL DÚIN BUILDS A CURRACH AND SETS SAIL

Before he did anything else, Máel Dúin went to the country of Corcomroe, to see Nuca the druid, to ask him for charms and blessings for the boat that he had decided to build.

The druid gave Máel Dúin some charms, and the blessings that he asked for. He told the youth on what day he should begin to build his boat, on what day to put out to sea, and how many men he should take with him; Máel Dúin was to take seventeen companions on his voyage – no more, and no less.

Trouble would follow the whole expedition if this instruction was disobeyed, Nuca warned.

On the appointed day, Máel Dúin set to building a large triple-hide currach. It was made of wickerwork, with eight thwarts and a strong mast, and it was covered with three layers of hard red ox-hide. He decorated the boat with the charms that Nuca had given him.

Then Máel Dúin gathered together the seventeen companions who would accompany him on his voyage. Among them were his good friends Germane and Diuran the poet.

Everything was ready by the time the day appointed by Nuca for their departure arrived.

They hoisted the sail to the mast, and put forth to sea. But they had gone only a little way when they heard the cries of Máel Dúin's three foster brothers, who had come running down to the beach, and were standing in the shallows, calling them back.

"You must go home!" Máel Dúin called over the waves. "I may not carry a larger number than are already with me! Nuca has spoken!"

"If you do not come back for us, we will follow you into the sea, even if we drown!" the foster brothers replied. And the three of them plunged into the water, and began to swim towards the currach.

When Máel Dúin saw this, he turned his vessel towards them, and took them on board, rather than let them be drowned. But his heart was heavy, for he remembered the druid's warning.

And they could not turn back, for the current and the wind were strong, and carried them away from the shore. They sailed all day, until finally the evening settled and turned into a long and dark night.

8. THE ISLAND OF THE RAIDERS

They kept rowing into the night, until at about midnight they came to two small and barren islands, on each of which was a fort.

Coming from the forts was the sound of a gathering. They could hear the noise of drunkenness and the commotion of warriors boasting of spoils won, along with the cries and moans of prisoners and hostages.

Máel Dúin and his crew set aside their oars and listened, and soon heard a loud voice, speaking proudly.

"Stand away from me, for I am a better man than you! It was *I* who slew the Eoganacht chief and burned the church of Dooclone over his head, and his kin have never dared to avenge it on me! Have *you* ever performed such a deed?"

The feelings that now seized Máel Dúin and his companions were fierce indeed!

"Now surely," said Germane and Diuran, "Heaven has guided us to this place! Here is an easy victory. Let us land and utterly destroy these forts, since God has revealed our enemies to us so quickly, and delivered them into our hands!"

But even as they spoke, a wind arose from Heaven, and a great tempest suddenly broke upon them.

And they were driven powerlessly before the violence of the storm, all that night, and for all of the following day and night.

When finally the storm abated and the sky cleared, they were floating in the midst of a great and boundless ocean. They saw neither the islands they had left, nor any other land. They had no way of knowing where they were, or where they were going. They were lost.

"Take down the sail, and lay your oars aside, and let the currach drift before the wind, in whatever direction it pleases God to take us," Máel Dúin said.

So the crew lowered the sail and ceased their rowing.

Máel Dúin then turned to his foster brothers and spoke the painful truth.

"This is your doing," he said. "This evil has befallen us because we took the three of you into the currach. Because of you, we have violated the commands given to us by the druid Nuca. There are too many of us. We are cursed. Without doubt, more troubles will come because of this."

His foster brothers made no reply, but sat in silence, with their heads bowed.

9. THE ANTS

They drifted aimlessly for three days and nights, with no sign of land.

But early on the morning of the fourth day, before the sun had risen, they heard a sound in distance.

"It is the sound of waves against the shore," said Máel Dúin.

When the sun rose and the day brightened, they rowed towards the noise and soon seeing an island, approached the shore.

Lots were cast among the crew to decide which of them should explore the strange land; but even as they were making ready to leave the boat, a great swarm of ants appeared, and every ant seemed the size of a horse.

They swarmed down to the beach, into the very sea, and they swarmed in the air around the boat; and they were agitated. It was clear that they were intent on devouring both the men and their boat.

Máel Dúin and his men were alarmed; the ants were almost on them, and so they turned their vessel and with both oar and sail made as much speed as they could, away from the island.

For three more days and nights they did not cease rowing; and for all this time, there was no sight of land.

10. MANY BRIGHTLY COLORED BIRDS

IN THE EARLY HOURS OF THE FOURTH DAY after they had fled the island of the ants, they again heard the murmur of waves on a distant beach.

As the day dawned, they saw a large island, with high terraces all around it, rising one behind another. On the terraces grew rows of tall trees, on which were perched great numbers of large brightly-colored birds.

The crew were about to cast lots to decide who should visit the island and see whether the birds were dangerous, but Máel Dúin himself decided to go.

Taking a few companions, he went ashore, and they explored the island cautiously – all the time remembering the ants – but they found nothing to hurt or alarm them.

So they trapped some birds, and took them back to the ship as food.

11. THE BEAST THAT THREW STONES

For another three days they sailed without seeing land, and then on the fourth day, they came upon a huge island with wide and flat beaches.

As they approached it, they saw a huge creature standing on the beach, looking at them attentively. It was like a horse in shape; but its legs were like those of a dog, and it had great, sharp claws, on which it balanced precariously. It pranced and leaped around on the beach, as though it was overjoyed to see them.

Máel Dúin was unsure about this creature. Telling his companions to proceed with care, for the monster seemed to him to be intent on making mischief, he instructed the oarsmen to row slowly towards land.

Máel Dúin soon made his decision. "I do not like this beast. It is too pleased to see us. We should leave this island at once."

And he was right, for in its heart, the creature was intending to kill and eat the travelers as soon as they landed on its beach.

They turned away from island. When the monster realized that they were leaving, it began digging up large rocks, and hurling them at the vessel.

It was all the crew could do to get beyond its reach, and the boat almost capsized, but they persisted, and rowed with all their strength, and so eventually they escaped into the open sea.

12. THE DEMONIC HORSE RACE

After sailing for several more days, a broad, flat island came into view. The crew cast lots, and it fell to Germane to go and examine it, but he did not think the task a pleasant one, for thoughts of the gigantic ants and the great monster they had met on the other islands were still in his mind.

Then Diuran said to him:

"I will go with you this time, and the next time it falls to my lot to visit an island, you shall come with me."

So both of them went together.

They found the island to be large. Some distance from the shore they came to a broad green racecourse, in which they saw immense hoof-marks, the size of a ship's sail, or a large table. There were nut shells as large as helmets scattered about, and the remains of the huge nuts that had been partially eaten.

Although they could see no one, they found many marks and signs that showed that people of huge size had been employed there, at all kinds of work. There were remains of all kinds, monstrous in size.

It seemed as though the giants had gone plundering, and left their scattered spoil lying about.

Seeing these strange things, they became alarmed, and so they returned to the shore, and called their companions to come ashore and view them as well.

The others, when they had seen the racecourse and

all the signs of the giants, were also struck with fear, and so they quickly returned to their currach, and set sail.

They had got only a little way from the island when they saw dimly, as if through a mist, a vast multitude of people on the sea, of gigantic size and demonic look, rushing along the crests of the waves towards the island, all with a great outcry of noise and shouting.

As soon as this shadowy host of giants had landed, they went to the green, where they began a horse race.

The monstrous horses were swifter than the wind; and as they pressed forward in the race, the demonic multitudes raised a mighty shout like thunder, which reached the crew as clearly as if they were in the boat with them.

Máel Dúin and his men, as they sat in their currach, heard the strokes of the whips and the cries of the riders; and though the race was far off, they could easily understand the eager words of the spectators.

"See the gray!"

"See that chestnut horse!"

"Watch the horse with the white spots!"

"My horse leaps better than yours!"

After seeing and hearing these things, the crew sailed away from the island as quickly as they were able, into the open ocean, for they knew that they had just witnessed a gathering of demons more powerful than anything they could imagine.

13. THE PALACE OF SOLITUDE

Having left the demons to their horse racing, they sailed for a full week with no sign of land, and so they again began to suffer from lack of food and water.

Their hunger was great by the time they came upon a vast island which rose high out of the waves. On the shore, right on the water's edge, they found a large and splendid house. The house had two doors; one faced inland, opening onto a wide plain, and the other faced the sea.

The doorway that faced the sea was sealed with a great flat stone, and in this stone was an opening through which the waves, as they beat tirelessly every day, threw large numbers of salmon into the house.

The voyagers landed, and searched through the entire house without meeting any one.

They saw in one large room a rich and beautifully ornamented couch that seemed to be intended for the head of the house, and in each of the other rooms was a couch for three members of the family. There were three cups of crystal on a table beside each couch, and also food and drink.

Thankful, they ate and drank till they were satisfied, thanking God for having saved them from hunger and thirst, and then they rested on the comfortable couches.

The occupants of the house did not appear, and they decided to set sail again.

14. THE GREAT APPLE TREE

And now they were many days voyaging, and again they were soon without food and drink. So they suffered from hunger and thirst, until finally they came to an island with great cliffs all around it.

A single apple tree grew in the middle of the island. It was very tall, and its branches were exceedingly slender and of incredible length, so that they grew all over the hill, and covered the entire island, and hung over the cliffs and all the way down to the sea.

When they came near the island, Máel Dúin caught one of the branches in his hand and broke it off.

For three days and three nights the ship circled the island, but they could find no entrance, or any way through the cliffs, so they could not land.

During all this time Máel Dúin kept hold of the branch that he had broken off, and by the third day, a cluster of three apples had grown on it.

Each of the apples satisfied the hunger of the entire crew for forty days.

15. THE WONDROUS CREATURE

They had just finished the last of the apples when they came to the next island. It had a stone wall all round it.

When they came near the shore, an monstrous creature of vast size, with a thick, rough skin, sprang up from inside the wall, and began to run around and around the island. The creature seemed to Máel Dúin to be swifter than the rush of the cold wind in March!

When it had ended its race, the beast went to the top of the hill in the center of the island, and standing on a large, flat stone, began to perform some kind of exercise, as if this was its daily custom. It put its head down, threw its legs up in the air, and turned itself completely around and around inside its skin, with the bones and flesh all moving, while the skin remained at rest.

When it was tired of this exercise, it rested a little; and then it began turning its skin continually around its body, down at one side and up at the other, like a mill wheel; but the bones and flesh inside did not move.

After spending some time at this strange work, it leaped up and ran around the island again, as fast as the wind, as if to refresh itself.

Then it went back to the same spot, and this time, while the skin that covered the lower part of its body remained still, it whirled the skin of the upper part around and around like a millstone, while the flesh and bones inside remained unmoving.

It was in this manner that the creature spent all its time on the island.

When Máel Dúin and his crew saw the strange and horrible antics of the monster, they were seized with dread, and they fled as fast as they could, putting out to sea in great haste.

The monster, seeing them about to leave, ran down to the beach to seize the ship. It began to smite at them, and even when they were out of reach, sailing away, it cast and lashed after them with stones from the shore, flinging them with great force and excellent aim, accompanied by terrifying howls and unearthly screams.

One of the stones struck Máel Dúin's shield and went right through it, lodging in the keel of the currach.

After this, the voyagers got beyond the creature's range as quickly as they could, and they were happy to sail away and leave the island behind.

16. THE BLOODTHIRSTY HORSES

A WEEK LATER, a most beautiful island next came into view. On it they saw multitudes of large animals shaped like horses that were standing tightly packed together, one next to the other.

As they drew near, the voyagers watched as one of the creatures opened its mouth and tore a great piece out of the side of the animal that stood next it, bringing away skin and flesh, and causing blood to stream down its flanks and onto the ground.

Immediately after, another of the creatures did the same to the nearest of its fellows.

And then the voyagers saw that all the creatures on the island kept worrying and tearing at each other in this manner; so that the ground was covered far and wide with the blood that streamed from their sides. The entire island was soaked crimson with their blood.

So they left that island as quickly as they could, and were all in a state of desperation. They were all sad, and complaining of feeling feeble and weak; for they knew nothing about this strange world, or where they were going, or how they might find help, or a safe place to land.

They were lost, and utterly without hope.

17. THE FIERY SWINE

THEY SAILED FOR A LONG TIME, suffering again from hunger and thirst, and praying fervently for relief from their torment.

At last – when they were sunken into a state of despair, and were quite worn out with privation and hardship of every kind – they sighted land.

Before them was a large and beautiful island, covered with countless fruit trees bearing an abundance of gold-colored apples. Under the trees they saw herds of heavy, stout animals, of a bright red color, shaped somewhat like pigs – but as they came nearer, and could see more clearly, they realized with astonishment that the animals were all fiery, and that their bright color was caused by the red flames which penetrated and illuminated their bodies from the inside.

The voyagers observed several of the creatures approach one of the trees, and striking the trunk all together with their hind legs, they shook some of the apples loose, and proceeded to eat them.

In this manner the animals occupied themselves every day, from early morning until the setting of the sun. As dusk descended, they retired into deep caves, far below the ground, where they stayed until the next morning.

There were swarms of birds swimming on the sea, all around the island. From morning until noon, they swam away from the land, farther and farther out to sea; but at noon they turned round, and from then until sunset, they swam back towards the shore.

At sunset, when the fiery creatures had retired to their caves, the birds flocked onto the island, and had their own turn at eating the apples.

Máel Dúin proposed that they should land on the island, and gather some of the fruit, saying that it could not be any more difficult or dangerous for them than it was for the birds; so two of the crew were sent ashore to examine the island.

They found that the ground was hot beneath their feet, for the fiery animals, as they lay sleeping in their underground lairs, heated the earth; but the two scouts persevered, and returned to the boat with some fruit.

When morning came, the birds left the island and swam out to sea, and the fiery creatures, emerging from their caves, went among the trees and began to eat.

The crew remained in their currach all day; and as soon as the animals had gone into their caves for the night, and the birds had taken their place, Máel Dúin led his men ashore.

They plucked the apples till morning, and brought them on board, until they had gathered as much as they could stow on their vessel. And then, refreshed, they put to sea once more.

18. THE LITTLE CAT

AFTER SAILING FOR A LONG TIME, their store of apples failed them, and again they had nothing to eat or drink.

They baked under a hot and merciless sun, and the sea gave forth an evil stench which filled their mouths and noses, so that it was difficult to breathe.

They were mightily relieved when at last a small island with nothing but a large palace on it came into view. As they got closer, they could see that around the palace was a wall, entirely white, without any marks or flaws, as if it had been perfectly carved out of a single vast rock of pure chalk. Where it faced the sea, the wall was so high that it seemed almost to reach the clouds.

The gate in this outer wall was open. Máel Dúin and his men went ashore and entered the gate, and found that there were many fine houses, all also as white as snow, arranged around the ramparts of the wall.
The houses were facing inwards, so that they enclosed a central court, onto which all the houses opened.

They entered the largest and finest of the houses, and searched through it without meeting anyone.

On reaching the largest room, a magnificent hall, they found a small cat playing among square marble pillars which stood arranged in a row. The cat was leaping from the top of one pillar to the top of another; it seemed to be an endless game.

When Máel Dúin and the others entered the room, the cat looked at them intently for a moment, and then returned to its play, and took no further notice of them.

Looking around the room, they saw three rows of precious jewels decorating the walls, reaching from one door to the other. The first was a row of brooches of gold and silver, with their pins fixed to the wall, and their faces outwards. The second was a row of torques of gold and silver, each as big as the hoop of a cask. The third was a row of great swords, with ornate hilts of gold and silver.

Around the room were placed couches, all pure white and richly ornamented. Abundant food of various kinds was spread on tables, among which was a boiled ox and a roasted hog; and there were many drinking-horns, all full of good strong ale.

"Is it for us that this food has been prepared?" Máel Dúin asked, the question directed at the cat.

The cat ceased its playing, and looked at him calmly for a moment; then it returned to its play. Since the cat did not object, Máel Dúin told his companions that the dinner was indeed meant for them, and they all sat down, and ate and drank until they were satisfied, after which they rested, and slept soundly on the couches.

When they awoke, they poured what was left of the ale into their wineskins, and they gathered the remnants of the food to take away with them.

As they were about to go, Máel Dúin's eldest foster

brother said "I am going to bring one of those golden torques!"

"No, do not!" said Máel Dúin. "It is enough that we have been given food and rest. Bring nothing away, for it is certain that this house will have someone to guard it."

The foster brother, however, ignored Máel Dúin's words, and took down one of the torques and brought it away with him.

But the cat followed him, and overtook him in the middle of the court. It sprang on him like a blazing, fiery arrow, passed through his body, and in an instant burned him into a pile of ashes.

The cat then returned to the room, and, leaping up onto one of the pillars, sat quietly upon it, impassively, as if nothing had happened.

Máel Dúin turned back, bringing the torque with him, and, approaching the cat, he spoke some soothing words. Then he put the torque back in the place from which it had been taken.

Having done this, he collected the ashes of his foster brother, and, bringing them to the shore, sorrowfully cast them into the sea.

Then they all boarded the currach, and set sail.

They continued their voyage, grieving for their lost companion, but at the same time thanking God for His many mercies to them.

19. THE ISLAND OF SHEEP

ON THE MORNING OF THE THIRD DAY, they came to another island, which was divided into two halves by a wall of brass running clear across the middle. They saw two great flocks of sheep, one on each side of the wall; and all those on one side were black, while those on the other side were white.

A large man was dividing and arranging the sheep. He would pick up a sheep and throw it easily over the wall, from one side to the other. When he threw a white sheep among the black ones, it immediately became black, and when he threw a black sheep among the white ones, it was instantly changed to white.

The travelers were alarmed by what they saw.

"It is good that we know this," said Máel Dúin. "Let us now throw something onto shore, to see whether it changes color. If it does, then we shall avoid this island altogether!"

So they took a branch with dark bark, and threw it among the white sheep. No sooner did it touch the ground than it became white. Then they threw a branch with white bark among the black sheep, and it turned black in an instant.

"It is lucky for us," said Máel Dúin, "that we did not land on the island, for then our own color would have changed, just like the color of those branches!"

Relieved, they turned around and sailed away.

20. THE BURNING RIVER AND THE HERDSMAN

On the eighth day, a large, broad island came into view. On it was a herd of gracefully shaped animals that somewhat resembled deer; they were most handsome creatures that any of them had ever seen.

They killed one for food, but it was too heavy to carry to the boat, so they butchered and cooked it on the spot.

Towards the center of the island rose a high mountain, which they decided to ascend in order to view their surroundings. Germane and Diuran the poet were chosen for this task.

When the pair had advanced some distance towards the mountain, they came to a broad shallow river. Sitting down on the bank to rest, Germane dipped the point of his lance into the water. The tip was instantly burned off, as if the lance had been thrust into a fierce furnace. So they went no further in that direction.

On the other side of the river, they saw a herd of animals like great oxen, all lying down and seemingly asleep. A gigantic man was standing near them.

Germane began to strike his spear against his shield, amusing himself by trying to rouse the cattle.

"Why are you frightening the poor young calves in that manner?" roared the giant, his tremendous voice making the ground tremble.

Germane was astonished to learn that such large

animals were nothing more than calves. Instead of answering the giant's question, he replied "But if these are the calves, then where are their mothers?"

"On the other side of the mountain of course!" the giant herdsman replied, and after that he turned his back to them, and would say nothing more.

Germane and Diuran returned to their companions, and told them of what they had seen and heard.

Then they raised the sail, took to their oars, and left the island.

21. THE MILL

The next island they came to had a large mill on it. Near its door stood the miller; he was a huge, strong, and burly man. Both the mill and the miller were hideous, and malformed, and ugly to the eye.

Máel Dúin saw countless crowds of people with horses and carts laden with corn coming towards the mill; and they waited until their corn was ground, and then collected the flour and carried it away.

There were also great herds of cattle approaching the mill, covering the island as far as the eye could see. They were pulling wagons laden with every kind of wealth that is produced in the world.

All the corn, and all the wealth, and all the cattle, and all the carts – everything, all of it – the miller fed into the mouth of his mill so that it was ground into dust. The hideous machinery never stopped, and the miller never rested. Everything became dust.

Máel Dúin approached the miller, and asked him the name of the mill, and the meaning of the mysterious things that they had were seeing on the island.

"This is the Mill of Inver tre Kenand, and I am the Miller of Hell, my friend! All the corn of the world is ground here. And all the riches that the people of the world are dissatisfied with, or which they complain of, or which they begrudge each other, are sent here to be ground into dust, along with every precious article which the world covets, and every kind of wealth which men try to conceal from God. All these I grind in my mill, until they are a fine dust, and then it is all sent away forever."

And now Máel Dúin saw countless laden horses and people bending under the weight of heavy sacks of useless dust, and all were leaving the mill, forever.

And forever, without pause, the unground corn and riches kept arriving in an endless stream of carts, and forever the ground corn and riches were carried away in bulging sacks as an endless stream of dust.

The miller said no more after that, but turned around and went back to his endless work.

And the voyagers, with much fear and awe in their hearts, shuddered and crossed themselves, and then returned to their currach and sailed away as quickly as they could, wanting with every fiber of their being to be far away from this awful place.

22. THE ISLAND OF SORROW

THEY HAD SAILED FOR ONLY A FEW HOURS when they discovered another large island, on which there was a great multitude of people who had entirely black skin and clothes, and black head-dresses as well. They were all perfectly black, from head to foot. They kept walking about, sighing and weeping and wringing their hands, as if they were inconsolable, without taking pause or rest.

The crew cast lots, and it fell to Máel Dúin's second foster brother to go and examine the island. But when he went ashore and walked among the people, he also fell into deep sorrow, and began to weep and wring his hands, crying and wailing along with everyone around him.

Two of the crew went ashore to bring him back; but they were unable to find him among the crowd of mourners; and, what was worse, in a short time they too began to weep and lament like all the rest.

Máel Dúin then chose four more men to go and rescue the others, and he put weapons in their hands, and gave them these directions:

"When you land on the island, wrap your cloaks around your faces, so as to cover your mouths and noses, so you do not breathe the air of the island; and look neither to the right nor to the left, neither at the earth nor at the sky, but fix your eyes only on our own men, until you have laid your hands on them."

They did exactly as they were told, and soon found their two companions who had been sent after the foster brother. Quickly, they seized them and brought them back.

When these two were asked what they had seen on the island, and why they had begun to weep and wail, their only reply was:

"We cannot tell. We only know that we had to do what we saw others doing. We had no choice."

Of the foster brother, though, there was no sign. He was lost forever in the crowd of wailing, mourning people, forever stricken with grief.

And so the voyagers sailed on, burdened with hearts that were heavy on account of having to leave the second foster brother behind.

23. THE FOUR FENCES

The next island was divided into four large fields by four walls that met in its center.

The first was a wall of gold, the second a wall of silver, the third a wall of copper, and the fourth was a wall of clear crystal.

In the first of the four fields was a crowd of kings; in the second, there were queens; in the third, youths; and in the fourth, there were young maidens.

When the voyagers landed, one of the maidens came down to the shore to meet them. She led them to a house, where she entertained them and gave them food, which she served to them from a small vessel which never emptied. The food looked like cheese, but whatever taste pleased each man most was the taste that he found it to have; so it seemed to each of them that he was eating his own favorite food.

Then she gave them sweet ale from a flask which also never emptied, and the strength of it caused them all to fall into a deep sleep that lasted three days and three nights.

When they awoke on the morning of the fourth day, they found themselves on board their own currach, alone on the open sea; and there was no sign in any direction of either the maiden, or the island.

So they continued their voyage, wondering what had happened.

24. THE PALACE OF THE GLASS BRIDGE

They came next to a small island.

There was a palace on it, with a brass door, and there were brass chains and fastenings on the door, hung all over with little silver bells. In front of the door was a fountain, spanned by a bridge of glass, which led to the palace.

They walked towards the bridge, intending to cross it, but every time they stepped onto the bridge they were pushed backwards by some strange force, so that they fell to the ground.

They had begun to grow weary from their attempts when the door opened and a beautiful young woman emerged from the palace, with a large bowl in her hand. She lifted a glass slab from the bridge, and filled her bowl from the fountain. Then she rose, and turned to go back to the palace.

"This woman would do to keep house for Máel Dúin!" called Germane, loudly enough for her to hear.

"Máel Dúin, indeed!" she laughed scornfully, and she shut the door firmly after her.

They struck on the door to gain admittance, and they shook at the brass chains, but the tinkling of the silver bells was so soft and melodious that the voyagers soon fell into a deep and tranquil sleep, and they all slept soundly until the next morning.

When they awoke, they saw the same young woman

come out of the palace. She lifted the glass slab and filled her bowl, just as she had done the day before.

"This woman has certainly been sent to keep house for Máel Dúin!" called Germane.

"Oh, how wonderful this Máel Dúin must be!" she laughed in derision, as she firmly shut the brass door behind her.

They stayed in this place for a third night, and on the following morning, the maiden came forth, and again filled her bowl with water. And again, Germane called to her, and again she replied in the same way.

But on the next day, she emerged from the palace to the sound of the silver bells, and walked towards them, splendidly and beautifully dressed, with her yellow hair bound by a circlet of gold, and wearing silver shoes on her feet. She had a white cloak over her shoulders, which was fastened in front by a silver brooch studded with gold; and next to her soft, snow-white skin was a flowing garment of fine white silk.

"My love and greetings to you, Máel Dúin, and to your companions," she said. And she mentioned them all, one after another, calling each by his own name.

"My love to you all," she said. "All of us here knew long before now that you were coming to our island, for your arrival has been foretold among us."

Then she led them to a large mansion standing by the sea, and there they found that their currach had been drawn high up onto the beach.

In the mansion she led them to a room full of couches, so that there was one for Máel Dúin alone, and there was also a couch for every three of his men.

The woman then served them, from one vessel, a food which was like bread; first to Máel Dúin, and then she gave a share to his companions; and whatever taste each man wished for, that was the taste he found. Just as on the island with the four fences, every man thought that he was eating his own favorite food.

Then she lifted the glass slab in the bridge, filled her bowl, and gave water to each of them; and she knew exactly how much to give, of both food and drink, so that each man had enough to be satisfied, and no more.

"This woman would indeed make a fine wife for Máel Dúin," said the voyagers to each other. But even as they spoke, she had returned to the palace.

Máel Dúin's companions gathered around him. "Shall

we ask this maiden to become your wife?" they asked.

"How could it hurt for you to speak with her?" Máel Dúin replied.

Next morning when she appeared, they said to her:

"Will you not stay here with us? Will you make a friend of Máel Dúin – and will you take him as your husband?"

She replied that she and all those that lived on the island were forbidden to marry the sons of men; and she told them that she could not disobey, as she did not know what sin or transgression was.

She then returned to her palace; and on the next morning, she returned. After she had served them food and drink as usual, until they were satisfied, and were relaxed, they again put the same questions to her.

"Tomorrow," she smiled, "you will get an answer to these questions of yours." And so saying, she went back across the glass bridge.

They were soon asleep on their couches.

When they awoke the following morning, they found themselves lying in their currach. It was sitting on a crag of rock surrounded by water. When they looked about, they saw neither the woman, nor the palace, nor the glass bridge – there was no trace anywhere of the island.

Without saying a word, they pulled their currach into the water, and sailed on.

25. THE SHOUTING BIRDS

ONE NIGHT, SOON AFTERWARDS, they heard in the distance a confused murmur of voices, as if there was a great choir singing psalms, or chanting.

Intrigued, they followed the direction of the sound, and at noon the next day, they came to an island that was covered with tall hills.

There were birds everywhere, in trees, and on the ground. Some were black, some red, and some speckled, and they were all shouting and speaking with human voices; it was from them that the great clamor was coming!

The tumult of chattering was so loud that the crew could not understand any of the speech; and the noise was so disturbing, and so loud, that none of the voyagers could tolerate it.

They sailed away without landing, happy to be away from the cacophony.

26. THE HERMIT

THE VERY NEXT DAY, they found a small island. This one had many trees on it – some standing alone, and some in clusters – on which, again, were perched great numbers of birds, but this time they made no sound.

They also saw an old man on the island, with long white hair and a beard so long that it almost touched the ground. They landed, and greeted him, asking who he was, and where he was from.

"I am from Erin," the old man replied. "One day, a long time ago, I put out to sea in a currach, meaning to embark on a pilgrimage; but I had not gone far when my currach suddenly became unsteady, as if it was about to overturn.

So I returned to land, and, in order to steady my boat, I placed under my feet at the bottom of my boat some green sods of grass, cut from one of the fields of my own farm, and then I began my voyage anew.

"Thanks to the guidance of God, I arrived at this spot; and He fixed the sods in the sea for me, so that they formed a small island. At first I had barely room to stand; but every year, from that time to the present, the Lord has added one foot to the length and breadth of my island, until finally, after the passing of many ages, it has grown to its present size.

"And on one day each year, the Lord has caused a single tree to spring up, until the island has become covered with trees. Now, I am so old that my hair has become pure white, and is almost long enough to reach the ground.

"And the birds that you see on the trees," he continued, "these are the souls of my children, and of all my descendants, both men and women, who are sent to this island when they die in Erin.

"The Lord has caused a well of ale to spring up for us on the island; and every morning angels bring me half a cake, a slice of fish, and a cup of ale from the well; and in the evening the same food and ale is dealt out to each of my flock.

"And it is in this manner that we live, and shall continue to live until the end of the world; for all of us here await the Day of Judgment."

Máel Dúin and his companions enjoyed the hospitably of the old hermit for three days and three nights. On the fourth morning, as they were leaving, he said to them:

"All of you will return to your country and your homes, except one. One of you will never see his home again."

27. THE MIRACULOUS FOUNTAIN

A FEW DAYS LATER, they found another island.

It was encircled by a golden rampart, and within the walls, the ground everywhere was as white as snow.

There was another old man there, and his hair was grown so much and so long that it covered him entirely. The island seemed to be quite bare, so Máel Dúin asked him how he fed himself.

"There is a fountain in this island," the old man replied. "On Fridays and Wednesdays, whey and water flow from it. On Sundays and on the feasts of martyrs, there is good milk. But on the feasts of the apostles, and of Mary and John the Baptist, we receive ale and wine."

And then every man was brought a cake and a piece of fine fish; and they drank their fill of the liquor from the island's fountain. The drink cast them into a heavy and unbroken sleep, which lasted until the following morning.

When they had passed three days and nights in this fashion, the hermit told them that it was time to go.

So they bade him farewell, and went on their way.

ð

28. THE BLACKSMITHS

WHEN THEY HAD BEEN roughly tossed about by the waves for a week or more, they were relieved to see land in the distance.

As they came near the shore, they heard the roaring of a great bellows, and the thundering sound of smiths' hammers striking a large glowing mass of iron on an anvil; and every blow seemed to Máel Dúin as loud as if a great crowd of men had brought down their hammers all at once.

Then, across the water, they heard the heavy, booming voices of the smiths in conversation.

"Are they close at hand?" a voice asked from inside the great smithy.

"They are!" replied a smith who was standing in the doorway of the smithy, observing the currach as it approached their island.

"Who is it that approaches?" asked a third voice.

"Why, it is a gaggle of little boys, in a cockleshell!"

When Máel Dúin heard this, he turned to the crew.

"Put back at once, but do not turn the currach! Reverse the sweep of your oars, and let her move stern first, so that these giants will not realize that we are fleeing!"

The crew obeyed straight away, for they too had heard the voices, and the currach began to move away from the shore, stern first.

The first voice spoke again. "Are they near the shore?" he asked the one who was watching. "Are they near the harbor?"

"They seem to be at rest," answered the other, "for I cannot see that they are coming closer, and yet they have not turned their little boat around!"

Their voices rolled across the water like thunder.

A short time later, the first voice asked "And what are they doing now?"

"It seems," replied the other, "that they are fleeing! They are further off now than they were a moment ago!"

At this, the owner of the first voice rushed quickly out of the forge. He was a massive, burly giant, and he held in a great pair of tongs a massive ingot of iron, still sparkling and glowing red from the furnace.

Running down to the shore with long, heavy strides that shook the ground, he flung the red-hot mass with all his might at the fleeing currach.

It fell short, plunging into the water just near the prow, causing the whole sea to hiss and boil, heaving up around the boat.

The voyagers leaned into their oars, and rowed for all they were worth, so that they quickly got beyond his reach, and out into the open ocean.

Greatly relieved, and safe, they sailed on.

29. THE SEA OF GLASS

The next day, they came to a sea which was as clear as green glass. It was so calm and transparent that the gravel and sand at the bottom were perfectly visible, sparkling in the sunlight.

And in this sea they saw neither monsters, nor any animals or fish, nor any rough rocks or reefs.

There was nothing but clear water and iridescent sand, and through it all, bright sunshine sparkled.

For a whole day they sailed over the sea of glass, spellbound by its splendor and beauty.

30. THE COUNTRY BENEATH THE WAVES

After leaving the sea of glass, they came to another sea. This one seemed like clear, thin cloud.

It was so transparent, and appeared so light, that they thought at first that it would not support the weight of the currach, and that they might fall from the surface, down through the drifts of light mist, until they reached the ocean floor.

Looking down, they could see, in the depths of the clear water, the most beautiful country that any of them had ever laid eyes on. They gazed down in wonder at the roofs of mansions and castles, surrounded by beautiful groves and woods.

In one place stood a single large tree. Sitting in its branches was a beast, fierce and terrible to look upon.

Around the tree, a great herd of oxen grazed. A man stood nearby, guarding them. He was armed with a shield, a spear, and a sword; but even so, when he looked up and saw the monster among the branches of the tree, he cried out, and turned and fled, as fast as his legs could carry him.

Then the monster stretched forth its neck, and darting its great head downward, plunged its fangs into the back of the largest ox in the herd. It lifted the screaming beast off the ground and up into the tree, where it swallowed it down in the twinkling of an eye. The rest of the herd took to flight, bellowing in panic.

When Máel Dúin and his people saw this, they were seized with terror; for they were afraid that they would not be able to cross the sea above the monster, on account of the extreme lightness and thinness of the water here.

And so although they continued on their way, on account of the danger they were careful – more careful than they had been at any time since they left their homeland.

They traveled slowly, and quietly, and the monster did not notice them, so that eventually they made their way safely across the country beneath the waves.

¶

31. A PROPHECY

WHEN THEY CAME TO THE NEXT ISLAND, they were astonished to see that it was below them, and that the sea rose up over it on every side, in sheer high walls.

It was as if the island lay at the bottom of a vast well, made somehow of the water itself, so that the crew looked down on the island from a great height, from the top of the great wall of water that surrounded it.

When the people of the island saw the voyagers far above them, they rushed about in a panic, shouting, "They are here! They have come, to despoil us and destroy us, as it has been said! They have come!"

Then the crew saw great numbers of men and women, all shouting and in great consternation, fleeing, and driving herds of horses, cows, and sheep before them.

A woman began to pelt them from below with large nuts, with acorns, and walnuts; she flung them so that they fell harmlessly onto the waves around the boat, where they remained floating. The crew gathered great quantities of them, and kept them for eating.

When they had finished gathering the nuts, they turned the currach to the open sea and began to row away. When the islanders below saw this, the shouting ceased, and there was silence; it was an apprehensive calm.

Then they heard one man ask "What are they doing

now?" and another answered him, "They are going away! They are leaving!", and a third voice said "Thank God! We are saved!"

From what Máel Dúin saw and heard at this island, it seemed to him that it had been prophesied among the people that their island would some day be spoiled and brought down by raiders; and that they thought that Máel Dúin and his men were the very enemies that they had been expecting.

But they were not those raiders, and they sailed on.

32. THE ARCH OF WATER

AFTER A FEW DAYS, they arrived at another island, and here was yet another strange thing.

A great stream of water rose up in a column out of the sand on the beach. It arched like a rainbow over the whole of the island, until it descended onto the beach on the other side.

The water was solid, like a beam, and the crew could pass beneath the arch without getting wet. And then when night came and they lay down on the ground to sleep beneath it, they remained dry.

In the morning, they pierced the arch with their spears, and through the holes they made, huge salmon came tumbling out in such vast numbers that the whole island was soon filled with the smell of the fish, for there were too many fish for the crew to gather them all.

For two days, they watched as the column of water never ceased to flow, and it never changed its place, or altered in any way, but remained spanning the island like a solid bow of water.

Then the voyagers, having filled their currach with all it could hold of the largest salmon, left the island, and sailed out into the open sea.

33. THE SILVER PILLAR

Then they traveled on, until they came to an immense column made entirely of silver, standing all alone in the ocean.

It had eight sides, each of which was the width of an oar-stroke of the currach. It rose out of the sea without any land or earth around it; there was nothing but the boundless ocean, so that water lapped against its sides. They could not see its base deep down in the water; it disappeared into the depths. Neither were they able to see the top, on account of its vast height. Above them, it reached into the sky until it disappeared.

A net made of woven silver had been hung from somewhere high above, and it reached down to the very water, where it extended far out from one side of the pillar; and the mesh was so large that the currach, in full sail, easily passed through it.

As they were sailing through it, Diuran struck the net with his sword, and cut a piece from it.

"Stop, do not damage the net," said Máel Dúin, "for this is the work of great men!"

"This," answered Diuran, holding up the piece of the net that he had cut off, "is for the honor of God! So that the story of our adventures might be believed, I shall place it as an offering on the altar at Armagh, if we ever reach our home again!"

That piece of the silver net weighed twenty ounces,

when it was weighed afterwards by the people of the church of Armagh.

After this, they heard someone speaking from far above them, in a loud, clear, and distinct voice; but they could not decipher either what was said, or in what language it was said.

They sailed on.

34. THE PEDESTAL

THE ISLAND THEY SAW AFTER THIS was named Encos (or One Foot), because it was suspended on a single massive pillar. They rowed all round it, looking for some entrance; but they could find no place to land.

However, deep down below the surface of the water, they saw a door that appeared to be securely closed and locked, and they thought that this must be the way into the pillar.

They could see a crowd of people on the island above them, and they called out, trying to attract their attention, but no one noticed them, and there was no reply.

So they left without conversing with anyone, and put out to sea once more.

35. THE ISLAND OF WOMEN

TEN DAYS LATER they came to a large island; on one side of it rose a lofty, smooth, heath-clad mountain. The rest of the island was a wide grassy plain.

Near the seashore stood a great tall palace, adorned with carvings and precious stones, and surrounded by a high wall.

They landed on the shore, and made their way towards the palace, where they sat to rest in front of an open gateway in the outer wall.

Looking through the gate, they saw seventeen beautiful young maidens, mingling, and laughing, and talking.

After they had sat for some time, a horse and rider appeared at a distance, coming swiftly towards the palace. As they approached, the travelers saw that the rider was a woman. She was beautiful, and richly dressed. She wore a blue, rustling silk head-dress, and a gold-fringed purple cloak hung from her shoulders. Her dress was embroidered with gold thread, and she wore black leather boots.

One of the maidens came out from the palace and held the horse as the woman dismounted and entered the palace. Soon after she had gone in, another of the maidens approached Máel Dúin and his companions.

"You are most welcome here," the maiden said. "Come into the palace; the Queen has sent me to invite you, and she is waiting to receive you."

They followed the maiden into the palace. She led them to a throne room, and here they found the woman that they had seen riding the horse.

The Queen welcomed them, and received them kindly. Then, leading them into a large hall in which a great dinner was laid out, she invited them to sit down and eat.

Dishes of rich food and a crystal goblet of wine were placed before Máel Dúin, and food and drink were laid before his companions, with each man being seated beside one of the maidens.

Having eaten and drunk until they were satisfied, they went to sleep on soft couches, each man with a woman, and Máel Dúin lay with the Queen.

The next morning, the Queen addressed Máel Dúin and his friends.

"Stay now in this country, and do not go wandering any longer over the wide ocean, from island to island. Here, old age or sickness will never come upon you. You will be always as young as you are at present, and you will live forever a life of ease and pleasure."

"Please, tell us," asked Máel Dúin, "how do you live here?"

"That is an easy question," answered the Queen. "The good King who formerly ruled over this island was

my husband, and these young maidens that you see are our children. He died after a long reign, and as he left no son, I took the throne. And every day I go among my people, to administer justice and to decide cases, for I am their Queen."

"Will you go there today?" Máel Dúin asked.

"Yes, I must go now," she replied. "I will give judgments among my people; but you can all stay in my palace until I return in the evening, and you need not trouble yourselves with any labor or care."

And so they remained there not just for the day, but for the three months of winter. And these three months appeared to Máel Dúin's companions to be as long as three years, and eventually, they began to want to return to their native land. One of them said to Máel Dúin:

"We have been a long time here; why do we not return to our own country?"

"What you say is neither good nor sensible," answered Máel Dúin, "for we shall not find in our own country anything better than we have here!"

But this did not satisfy his companions, and they began to murmur loudly.

"It is quite clear," they said, "that Máel Dúin loves the Queen of this island; and as this is so, let him stay here; but as for us, we shall return to our own country."

Máel Dúin, however, would not stay without them, so he told them that he would go with them.

One day, not long afterwards, when the Queen had

gone to administer justice as was her custom, they prepared their currach and put out to sea.

They had not gone far from land when the Queen came riding towards the shore. Seeing them sailing away, she hurried to the palace and returned with a ball of twine in her hand.

Riding down to the water's edge, she flung the ball after the currach, but held the end of the twine in her hand. Máel Dúin caught the ball, and it clung to his hand; and the Queen, pulling the twine towards her, drew the currach back to the very spot from which they had set out.

When they landed, she made them swear that if this happened again, someone would always stand up in the boat and catch the ball.

So the voyagers stayed on the island, much against their will. And every time they attempted to escape, the Queen brought them back by the same means, with Máel Dúin always catching the ball.

After what could have been months, or years (no one could tell), the travelers held council, and this is what they said:

"We know now that Máel Dúin does not wish to leave the island; for he loves this Queen very much, and he catches the ball of twine whenever we try to escape, so that we are forever brought back to the palace."

Máel Dúin heard this, and he replied "Then let some one else catch the ball next time, and let us see whether it will cling to his hand as it does to mine."

They agreed to this, and at the next opportunity, they again put off towards the open sea. The Queen arrived, as usual, before they had gone very far, and flung the ball after them, as before.

Another member of the crew caught it, and it clung as firmly to his hand as it had to Máel Dúin's, and the Queen began to draw the currach towards the shore.

But Diuran, drawing his sword, cut off the man's hand, and it fell with the ball of twine into the sea, and sank out of sight.

The men gladly leaned into their oars, and the currach sped away from the island.

When the Queen saw this, she began to weep and lament, wringing her hands and tearing her hair with grief; and her maidens also began to weep and cry aloud.

The whole palace, and the whole island, was full to the brim with grief and lamentation, and the sound carried across the water, so that Máel Dúin and the others could hear every sob and cry as easily as if the women were in the boat with them.

Even though the men were stricken with heavy hearts at hearing this, they were resolved, and doubled their efforts, and so finally made good their escape from the island.

§

36. THE FRUIT

For a long time, they were thrown about on high waves that were whipped up by strong winds, but finally they came to an island that was covered with trees laden with masses of a fruit which the voyagers had never seen before; it was large, and not much different in appearance from apples, except that it had a rough skin, and red flesh.

After the crew had plucked all the fruit off one of the trees, they cast lots to decide who should try eating it, and the task fell to Máel Dúin.

So he took some of the fruit, and, squeezing the juice into a cup, drank it. It threw him quickly into a sleep so deep that he seemed to be in a deep trance rather than a natural slumber, without breath or motion, and with the red juice staining his lips.

Until the same time the next day, no one could tell whether Máel Dúin was alive or dead, and fear spread through the crew.

When he awoke next day, he told the others to gather as much of the fruit as they could bring away with them; for the world, he told them, had never produced anything so wonderful and sweet!

They pressed the fruit until they had filled all their jars and wineskins with juice, and then they sailed on.

37. THE THREE EAGLES

A WEEK LATER, they landed on another large island. On one side, it was overgrown with great forests of yew and oak; and on the other was a broad flat plain, in the middle of which was a small lake, with herds of sheep feeding in the surrounding meadows.

There they also saw a church and a fortress. They entered the church and found there an old monk, ancient and gray.

Máel Dúin asked him who he was, and where he came from.

"I am the fifteenth and last man of the community of the blessed Brendan of Birr," the old cleric replied. "We went forth on a pilgrimage into the vast and boundless ocean, and we came to this island. And of the fifteen men, all have died here but me."

Then he showed them the tablet of the blessed Brendan, which they had taken with them on their pilgrimage. The travelers bowed reverently before it, and Máel Dúin held it with great devotion and kissed it.

"You may stay here as long as you wish," said the old man, "and eat your fill of the sheep for food, but take no more than is necessary to satisfy your hunger."

So they stayed there for a season, and fed well on the flesh of the sheep, and they worshiped with the cleric.

One day, as they were seated on a hill, gazing out over the sea, they saw what looked like a black cloud coming towards them from the south. They kept watching as it came nearer and nearer; and at last they realized with amazement that it was an immense bird, for they could see quite plainly the slow, heavy flapping of its huge wings.

When it reached the island, it alighted on a hill next to the lake; and they were alarmed, for they thought, on account of its vast size, that if it saw them it might seize them in its talons, and carry them off across the sea.

So they hid themselves under trees and among rocks, but they never lost sight of the bird, for they were determined to watch its movements.

The bird appeared to be old, and weary. It held in one claw a branch, which it had carried with it from over the sea. The branch was larger and heavier than the largest full-grown oak on the island, and was covered with fresh green leaves and heavy clusters of red and rich-looking fruit that resembled grapes; but they were much larger.

It remained resting for some time on the hill, being weary after its flight, and then it started eating the fruit off the branch. After watching it for some time, Máel Dúin crept warily towards the hill, to see whether the creature was inclined to make mischief; but the bird showed no disposition to do harm. This encouraged the others, and they followed their leader.

The whole crew now marched in a body around the bird, headed by Máel Dúin, with their shields raised; and as it still made no movement, one of the crew went

straight up to the bird, and brought away some of the fruit from the branch which it held in its huge talons. The bird went on plucking and eating the fruit, and never took the least notice of the theft.

On the evening of that same day, as the men sat looking over the sea to the south, where the great bird had first appeared to them, they saw in the distance two other birds, just as large, coming slowly towards them from the same direction.

On they came, flying at a great height, nearer and nearer, until at last they swooped down and alighted on the hill, one on each side of the first bird.

Although they were plainly much younger than the other, they also seemed tired, and took a long rest.

Then, shaking their wings, they began picking at the old bird, plucking out its old feathers, and smoothing down its plumage with their great beaks. After this had gone on for some time, the three birds together began picking the fruit off the branch, and they continued to eat until they were satisfied.

Next morning, the two birds began again at the same work, picking and arranging the feathers of the old bird as before; and at midday they ceased, and began again to eat the fruit, throwing the stones and what they did not eat of the pulp into the lake, so that soon the water had turned as red as wine.

After this, the old bird plunged into the lake and remained in it, washing itself, until evening, when it again flew up onto the hill, but perched on a different part of it, to avoid touching and defiling itself with the old feathers and the other traces of age and decay which the younger birds had removed from it.

On the morning of the third day, the two younger birds set about arranging the old bird's feathers for the third time. On this occasion, they applied themselves to their task in a manner much more careful and particular than before, smoothing the plumes with gentle touches, and arranging them in graceful lines, and tufts, and ridges. And so they continued without the least pause until midday, when they ceased, apparently satisfied with their work.

Then, after resting, they opened their great wings, rose into the sky, and flew away towards the south, until the men lost sight of them in the distance.

Meanwhile the old bird, after the others had left, continued to smooth and plume its feathers until evening; then, shaking its wings, it rose up and flew three times around the island, as if trying its strength.

And now the men observed that it had lost all appearance of old age: its feathers were thick and glossy, its head erect, and its eye bright, and it flew with all the power and swiftness of the two younger birds.

Alighting for the last time on the hill, after resting a little, it rose again into the sky, and turning its flight after the other two, it was soon lost to view.

It was obvious to Máel Dúin and his companions that

this bird had undergone some renewal of its youth from old age, according to the word of the prophet: "Thy youth shall be renewed as the eagle."

On seeing this great wonder, Diuran was inspired, and he addressed the crew: "Let us also bathe in the lake, and we shall obtain for ourselves a renewal of our own youth, just like the bird."

But the others were afraid, and would not, and said, "No, for the bird has left the poison of its old age and decay in the water. It will do us harm."

Diuran, however, insisted on having his own way, and he told them that he was going to try the water, whether they followed his example or not; the rest of them, he proclaimed, could do as they pleased.

So he plunged in and sat in the water for some time, after which he took a little and mixed it in his mouth, and in the end, he drank some.

He emerged perfectly sound and whole; and he remained so afterwards. For as long as he lived, he never lost a tooth, nor had a single gray hair, and he suffered neither from disease, or bodily weakness of any kind. But none of the others dared to enter the water.

The voyagers, having remained long enough on this island, stored in their currach a large quantity of the flesh of the sheep, and after bidding a fond farewell to the old monk, they sought the ocean once more.

38. THE LAUGHING FOLK

THEY SAILED ON until they came to an island which had a great level plain extending over its whole surface, and on this plain a vast multitude of people were playing games and laughing, without ever stopping for rest.

The voyagers cast lots to decide who would go to examine the island, and the lot fell upon Máel Dúin's third foster brother.

But as soon as he set foot on the island, he too began to play and laugh, without ceasing. His comrades called him back, but in vain; he would not listen. He leaped, and laughed, and sang as though all his life he had been one of the islanders.

He never paused in his play and joyous laughter, and seemed to have no awareness at all of his crewmates.

So after waiting for a long time, and being afraid to venture onto the island themselves, they put forth again, even though they were sad beyond words to leave him.

And so, finally, the stage was set for the fulfillment of the prophesy of Nuca the druid – that only Máel Dúin and the seventeen appointed comrades would return in safety to the land of their birth.

39. THE WALL OF FIRE

They came next to a small island that was surrounded by a high wall of fire that rotated around the entire island like a wheel, endlessly, without pausing, without any deviation.

At one place in the wall was an arch, which was open, with no gate; and whenever this arch, as the wall of flames turned around the island, came to them, they had a clear view of the entire island, and everything on it.

They could see men and women there, all of them beautiful and glowing with health, and wearing rich garments and jewelry, and they were all feasting, and drinking from glorious golden cups.

The crew marveled at the beauty of the music that came floating across the water, and for some time they could do nothing but gaze upon this marvel, for it was so lovely that they did not want to leave, so full were their hearts with happiness and joy.

But still, there was something that prevented them from landing, although they did not know what it was. There was something here that they could not bring themselves to trust.

Eventually they sailed on, but with aching hearts.

40. THE MONK OF TORAIGH

THEY HAD NOT BEEN SAILING LONG when they sighted something a long way off towards the south.

At first they thought it was a large white bird floating on the sea, rising and falling with the waves; but on turning their currach towards it for a closer view, they found that it was a man!

He was old, with long, white hair, and was wearing a monk's robe. He was sitting quite alone on a bare rock surrounded by water, and he kept continually throwing himself onto his knees, and performing prostrations, and he prayed without ceasing.

When they saw that he was a holy man, they asked for his blessing, which he gave. Then they began to talk with him; they asked who he was, and how he had come to be all alone on this rock.

In reply to their many questions, here is the story that he told the travelers.

"I was born and bred on the island of Toraigh. When I grew up, I became the cook to the brotherhood of the monastery – and a wicked cook I surely was, for every day I sold part of the food entrusted to me, and with the money, I secretly bought many choice and rare things.

I did even worse than this; I made secret passages underground into the church and the houses belonging to it, and I stole from time to time great quantities of golden vestments, book covers adorned with brass and gold, and other holy and precious things.

I soon became wealthy, and my rooms were filled with costly furniture, I had clothes of every color, both linen and woolen, I had brazen pitchers and cauldrons, and brooches and armlets of gold. Nothing was wanting in my house, of furniture or ornament, that a person in a high rank of life might be expected to have. I became proud and overbearing.

One day, I was sent to dig a grave for the body of a rustic that had been brought from the mainland to be buried on the island.

I went and decided on a spot in the graveyard; but as soon as I had set to work, I heard a voice speaking, coming from deep in the earth beneath my feet:

Do not dig this grave!

I paused for a moment, in shock; but, recovering myself, I resolved to ignore the mysterious voice, and began to dig again. And the moment I did so, I heard the same voice, even more plainly than before!

Do not dig this grave! I am a devout and holy person, and my body is lean and light; do not put the heavy, foul body of that sinner down upon me, in my own grave!

"But" I answered, in a desperate excess of pride and obstinacy, "I will certainly dig this grave; and I will bury this body on top of you!"

If you put that body in my grave, the flesh will fall off your bones, and you will die, and you will be sent to the infernal pit after three days – and the body of that sinner will not remain where you put it!

"Then what will you give me," I asked, "if I do not bury this corpse on top of you?"

Everlasting life in heaven, replied the voice.

"How do you know this; and how am I to be sure of it?" I inquired.

And the voice answered me: *The grave you are digging is clay. Observe now whether it will remain so, and then you will know the truth of what I tell you. And you will see that what I say will come to pass, and that you cannot bury that man on me, even if you should try to do so!*

These words were scarcely said when the grave was turned into a mass of white sand before my eyes, and there was no clay to be seen.

When I saw this, I was shocked and afraid, and I took the body away and buried it somewhere else.

It happened, some time later, that I had an expensive new currach made, with the hides painted red all over; and I went out to sea in it. As I sailed around the shores and islands, I was so pleased with the view of the land and ocean from my currach that I resolved to live in it at sea; and so I brought on board all my treasures – my silver cups, gold bracelets, and decorated drinking horns, and everything else, from the largest to the smallest article.

I enjoyed myself at first, for the air was clear, and the sea was calm and smooth. Life was good, friends.

But one day, the wind suddenly rose, and a fierce storm burst upon me. My currach was carried far out to sea, so that I lost sight of land, and I had no idea in which direction I was being taken.

After several days, the wind abated, the sea became smooth again, and my currach sailed on peacefully.

But then, even though the breeze was still blowing, my currach ceased moving, and, looking around to find the cause, I saw with great surprise an old man not far off, sitting on the crest of a wave!

He spoke to me; and, as soon as I heard his voice, I knew it at once, but I could not at the moment recall where I had heard it before. And I became greatly troubled, and began to tremble, although I did not know why.

"Where are you going?" the old man asked.

"I do not know," I replied, "but this I do know –

I am pleased enough with the smooth, gentle motion of my beautiful currach over the waves, rather than having to endure the rough waters of storms and gales!"

"You would not be pleased," replied the old man, "if you could see the masses that are at this very moment swirling all around you!"

"What masses do you speak of, old man?" I asked.

"All the space around you, as far as you can see across the sea, and upwards to the clouds, is a great towering mass of demons, and they are here on account of your avarice, your thefts, your pride, and all your other crimes and vices." He paused. "Do you know why your currach has stopped?"

"No, I do not," I answered, looking around me and seeing no demons, yet in truth, I was feeling ill at ease.

"It has stopped because I willed it – and it will never move from this spot until you swear that you will do what I am about to require of you!"

I replied that perhaps it was not in my power to grant his demand – nor in his power to make it.

"It *is* in your power to do as I say," he answered. "And if you refuse me, the torments of hell await you!"

He came close to the currach, and, laying his hands on me, made me swear to do as he demanded.

"What I require is this," he said. "You are to throw into the sea, right now, this very moment, all the ill-gotten treasures that you have in this currach!"

This grieved me very much. "It is a great pity that all

these valuable things should be lost!" I replied.

"They will not be lost," he replied. "Someone will be sent to take charge of them. Now, do as I say!"

So, against my wishes, I threw all my beautiful and precious things overboard, keeping only a small wooden cup to drink from.

"You will now continue your voyage," he said, "and the first solid ground your currach reaches, no matter what and where it is, there you are to stay."

He then gave me seven small cakes and a flask of thin whey to sustain me on my voyage; after which the currach began to move, and soon I lost sight of him.

And then, all at once, I realized with horror that the old man's voice was the one I had heard when I was about to dig the grave for the dead rustic!

I was so astonished and troubled at this discovery, and so disturbed at the loss of all my wealth, that I threw aside my oars, and gave myself up altogether to the winds and currents, not caring where I went. For many days, I was tossed about on the waves, and I had no way of knowing where I would be taken.

At last it seemed to me that my currach ceased to move; but I was not sure about it, for I could see no sign of land. Mindful, however, of what the old man had told me – that I was to stay wherever my currach stopped – I looked round carefully; and at last I saw, near me, a small rock, over which the waves were gently laughing and tumbling.

As I had been instructed, I stepped on to the rock. At the moment I did so, the waves seemed to spring back, and the rock rose high above the level of the water. My currach drifted away and soon disappeared, and I never saw it again. This lonely rock has been my home ever since.

For the first seven years, I lived on the seven cakes and the whey that the monk had given to me. At the end of that time the cakes were all gone; and for three days I fasted, with nothing but the whey to wet my mouth.

Late in the evening of the third day, an otter brought me a salmon from the sea, but although I suffered much from hunger, I could not bring myself to eat the fish raw, and it was soon washed back into the waves.

I remained without food for three more days, and on the afternoon of the fourth day, the otter returned with the salmon. And I saw another otter bring firewood; and when he had piled it up on the rock, he blew on it until it burst into flames. And then I cooked the salmon, and ate until my hunger was satisfied.

The otter continued to bring me a salmon every day, and I lived here for seven more years. The rock also grew larger every day, until it became the size you now see it.

At the end of the seven years, the otter ceased to bring me salmon, and so I fasted again. On the third day, I was sent half a cake of fine flour and a slice of fish; and on the same day my cup of whey fell into the sea, and another cup of the same size, filled with fine dark ale, was placed on the rock beside me.

And so I have lived, praying and doing penance for my sins, to this day. Each day my cup is filled with ale, and I am sent half a wheat cake and a slice of fish; and neither rain nor wind, nor heat, nor cold, is allowed to torment me on this rock."

And this was the end of the old man's story.

In the evening of that day, each man of the crew received the same quantity of food that was sent to the old hermit himself – half a cake and a slice of fish – and each man had as much good ale as he needed.

The next morning, the hermit had more to say to them.

"You will all return safely to your own country. And you, Máel Dúin, shall find on an island on your way the very man who slew your father; but you are neither to kill him, nor take revenge on him in any way.

"As God has delivered you from the many dangers you have passed through, even though you are guilty of so many sins, so too you are to forgive your enemy for the crime he has committed against you. And now, my friends, it is time for you to go home."

On hearing this, with fond farewells they took leave of the old monk, and sailed away.

41. THE FALCON

Soon after they left the hermit, they saw a lush and beautiful island, covered with rich grassland, and with herds of oxen and sheep browsing over its hills and in its valleys; but there were no houses, nor inhabitants, to be seen anywhere.

And so they stayed here for some time, and ate their fill of beef and lamb.

One day, while they were resting on a hill, a large falcon flew across the island.

One of the crew cried out: "See that falcon! He is surely like the falcons of Erin!"

"Let us watch him closely," said Máel Dúin, "and see in which direction he flies."

And so they watched the falcon, and they saw that he flew off to the south-east, without turning or wavering.

They went to their currach, and set out to the south-east, following the path of the falcon. They rowed the whole day, and just as dusk was settling, an island appeared on the horizon.

42. THE HOMECOMING

As they approached the island, they recognized it as the very same one which they had seen at the beginning of their voyage, on which they had heard the voice of a man boasting that he had slain Máel Dúin's father, and from which the storm had driven them out into the great ocean.

They had returned to the beginning point of their long, strange voyage!

They turned their vessel towards the shore, and were soon standing on a beach which seemed familiar. And there, in front of them, was the same house that they had seen such a long time ago. They walked towards it, wondering what this all meant.

Now, it so happened that the people of the house were seated at their evening meal; and Máel Dúin and his companions, as they gathered outside, could clearly hear their conversation.

"It would not go well for us if we were to see Máel Dúin now," a voice said.

"Ha! Máel Dúin!" answered another. "It is well known that he and his friends were drowned at sea long ago!"

"Do not be sure," cautioned a third voice. "He could be the very man that wakes you one morning from your sleep, with vengeance in his heart!"

"Supposing he came now!" exclaimed another.

"What would we do?"

The head of the house now spoke in reply to that last question; and Máel Dúin instantly recognized the voice of his father's killer.

"I can answer that," the voice said. "Máel Dúin has been for a long time suffering great afflictions and hardships; and if he were to come here now, though we were enemies once, I should certainly offer him welcome, and a kind reception."

When Máel Dúin heard this, his heart melted, and he was glad and full of forgiving, and he knocked at the door. The door-keeper came and asked who was there.

"It is I, Máel Dúin," he replied, "and I have returned safely with my friends from our wanderings."

The chief of the house ordered the door to be opened. He came to meet Máel Dúin, and he himself brought the traveler and his companions into the house.

They were all joyfully welcomed by the household; new garments were given to them, and they feasted and rested, until they forgot their weariness and their hardships, and there was no longer any bitterness or resentment left in any heart.

And then they told their stories, about all the marvels that God had shown them, all the people that they had met, and the creatures that they had encountered.

After they had remained there for some days, Máel Dúin and his friends returned in peace to their own country, having made many new friends.

Then Máel Dúin returned to his own home and his people, where he was received with love and joy.

Diuran the poet took with him the piece that he had cut from the net at the silver pillar. He laid it on the high altar of Armagh as he had promised, with thanks for the many miracles that the Lord had shown them.

And for the rest of their lives, Máel Dúin and his friends would tell the stories of everything that had befallen them, all the marvels they had seen, all the wisdom they had gained, and all the perils from which they had been protected by the Grace of God.

Let it be known that Aed the Fair, the chief sage of Ireland, laid down this story as it appears here. He did so as a delight to curious minds, and for the benefit of all the people who came after him.

DEIREADH MAR SIN AN SGÉAL

THE END

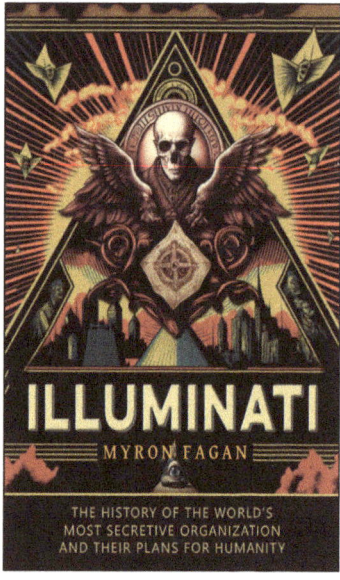

X@ADISTANTMIRROR.COM

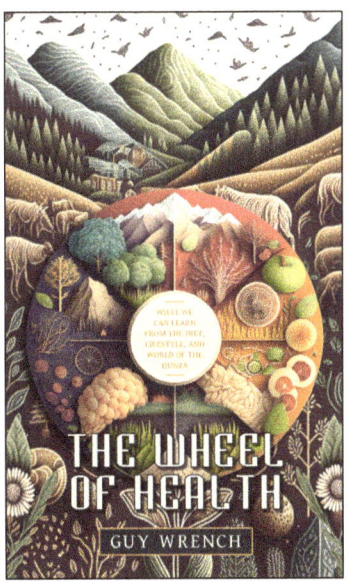

SEE MORE AT ADISTANTMIRROR.COM

www.ingramcontent.com/pod-product-compliance
Lightning Source LLC
Chambersburg PA
CBHW051538010526
44107CB00064B/2764